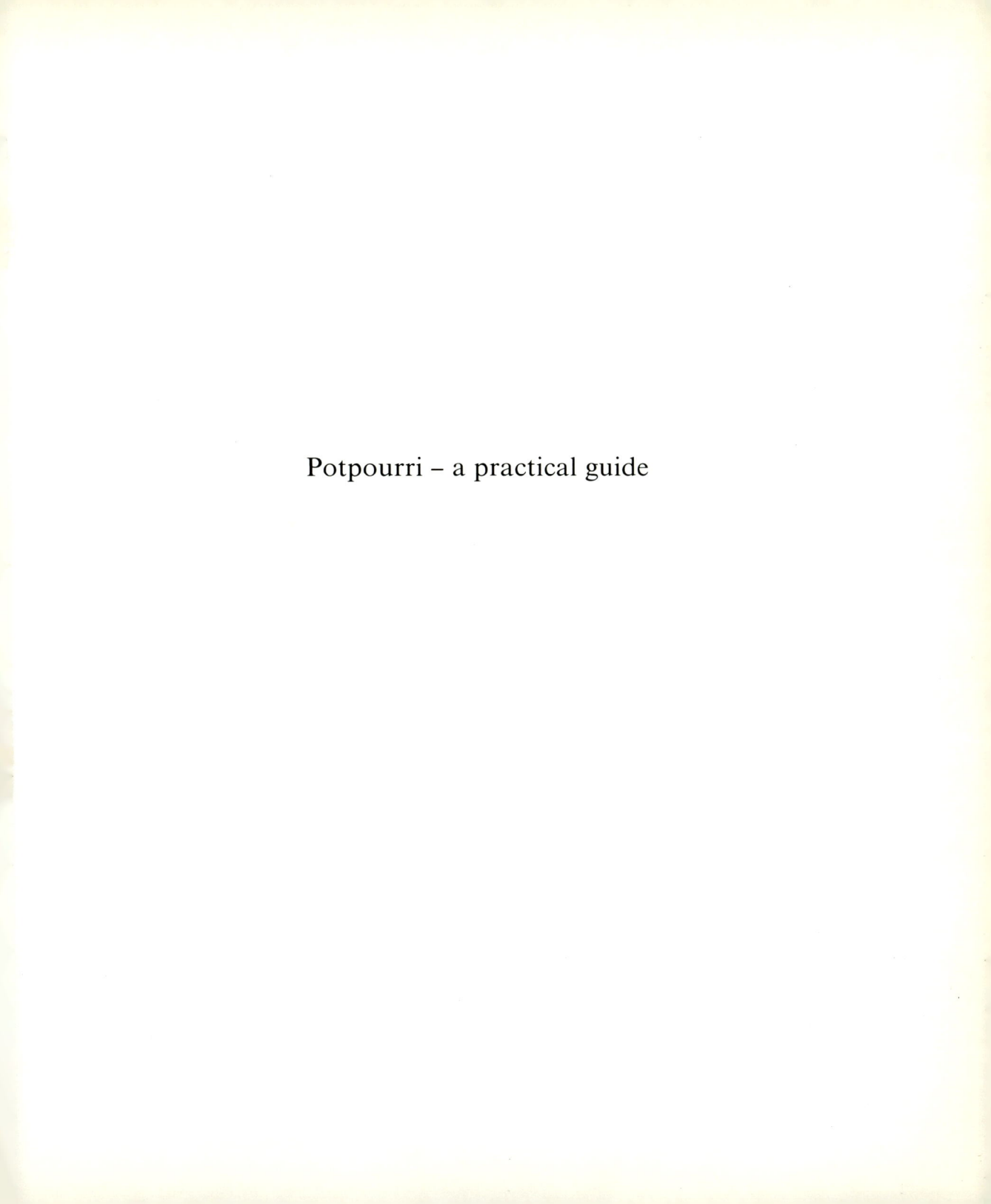

Potpourri – a practical guide

An arrangement of fragrant flowers and herbs

Potpourri
– a practical guide

Mary Lane

Bishopsgate Press Ltd
37 Union Street, London, SE1 1SE

Acknowledgements

I wish to thank Mrs King of Lullingstone Castle, Iden Croft Nurseries and Herb Farm, Hollington Nurseries Ltd., David Austin Roses and Peter Beales Roses for their kind permission to use photographs of their flowers, plants and gardens. I would also like to thank The Herb Society for allowing the use of their library for research and for their helpful advice.

ISBN 0 900 873 69 8 (cased)
      0 900 873 70 1 (limp)

British Library Cataloguing in Publication Data

Lane, Mary
   Pot pourri : a practical guide.
   1. Perfumes   2. Flowers—Drying
   I. Title
   745.92   TP983

ISBN 0-900873-69-8
ISBN 0-900873-70-1 Pbk

© 1986 Mary Lane

All rights reserved. No part of this publication may be reproduced, stored in a retrieval system, or transmitted, in any form or by any means, electronic, mechanical, photocopying, recording or otherwise, without the prior permission of the copyright owner.

All enquiries and requests relevant to this title should be sent to the publisher, Bishopsgate Press Ltd., 37 Union Street, London, SE1 1SE

Printed by Whitstable Litho Ltd., Millstrood Road, Whitstable, Kent.

Contents

Introduction	7
Scented Gardens	8
Growing Scented Roses	10
Lavender	28
Other Flowers used in Potpourri	30
Aromatic Plants for use in Potpourri	36
Gathering and Drying	42
Potpourri Recipes	52
Using Potpourri	70
Flower Meanings	86
Reading	92
Suppliers	93
Gardens to Visit	94

1 *A delightful display of herbs compact enough to suit most gardens.*

Introduction

The art of making potpourri is as old as the art of cooking, and in the days before deodorants and chemists, it was in some ways almost as important. The use of potpourri in those days ranged from the simple use of sweet herbs strewn on the floor to the subtle blends of flowers, herbs and spices made to sweeten the air and thereby promote good temper, sleep, energy or even passion. Mixtures were also tried to combat ill health, plague, moths and other undesirables.

These days we have very efficient synthetic remedies for most ills, but this old art can still be beneficial as well as giving infinite pleasure.

While it is convenient to have a flower garden from which to gather scented petals and leaves it is not essential, as potpourri can also be gathered from hedgerows and woodland to become a scented reminder of a country walk or prunings of an ivy leafed geranium grown indoors in a pot may be dried and made into scented sachets.

While this book lists some of the well tried and traditional recipes, I have also included some more modern ones and some of my own favourites. I hope that the reader, using this book as a guide to the basic requirements of potpourri making, will be able to blend the scents which he or she personally finds most pleasing and derive pleasure, and maybe profit, from the harvest of flowers.

Scented Gardens

The oldest gardens known are herb gardens. Herbs were originally used both for eating and for healing; so those vitally important gardens were made as near the house as possible, often walled to keep out animals, paved to make picking easier in all weathers, and to contain the invasive herbs in the beds allocated to them.

These gardens were sometimes quite small, but the beds would have been cut in formal patterns by people who loved ornamentation. The central point of the garden was often a sundial.

Later the pleasure garden developed round the rose, sometimes larger and more elaborate than the herb garden, but still with beds cut in the same formal designs. Though these rose gardens might have been made around a fish pond and have been sheltered by a yew hedge instead of a wall. At this time gardeners began to draw attention to the design of these gardens by edging the beds with little box hedges or sometimes with clove pinks for a softer effect; but the roses were usually planted at set intervals in the bare earth and the effect was a little hard and not really natural to the eye. Today both roses and herbs are often planted together to form the scented garden, beautiful in itself but also useful for potpourri and cooking.

The prettily shaped beds traditionally used for these plants are still one of the best ways of displaying them and can be adapted in size and shape to suit any garden. The paths may be paved or grassed and the beds which need not be very large can be raised to give easier access.

2. *A border of herbs can be attractive as well as fragrant.*

2

Growing Scented Roses

Rose petals are the main ingredient of most potpourri recipes. There is a wonderful selection of scented roses, both old and new, from which to choose. I list below a selection that are easily obtainable from many nursery gardens and are popular for the making of potpourri.

Gallica Roses

R. gallica officinalis (The Apothecary's Rose) was found to retain its scent when dried and powdered. An industry sprang up around it in the 13th Century, the centre of which was at Provins in France. Rose conserves, rose water and ointments were made from the rose petals which were also sold in the dried form for their fragrance.

Most Gallicas flower once in a season, although a few of the later hybrids produce sporadic blooms up to the autumn. They have few thorns and grow 1–2 metres tall.

The Gallicas should be pruned annually, some old wood will need to be removed and the long growth cut back by about one third.

Belle de Crecy has fragrant deep pink double flowers maturing to violet.

Charles de Mills produces generous double flowers which are strongly scented and are cerise to dark purple in colour.

Officinalis (Apothecary's Rose, Red Rose of Lancaster) is a semi-double flower with red wavy petals and a marvellous scent.

Rosa Mundi is one of the oldest and best known roses. The flowers are striped and splashed with light red, pink, and white and are semi-double and fragrant.

Tuscany Superb has double well scented flowers with crimson velvet petals.

3. *The Gallica rose Charles de Mills, its scent and colour makes it ideal for potpourri.*

3

Damask Roses

This rose is thought to have been first brought to England by the crusaders returning from Damascus. Most Damask roses flower once only during the summer and have a rich scent. Damask roses do not need hard pruning but after flowering the plant should be gently pruned to retain the shape.

Madame Hardy is a beautiful old white rose, the flowers of which are very double and sweet smelling. It grows to 2 metres.

In general white rose petals dry to an uninteresting biscuit colour and do not enhance the look of potpourri, but this rose is worth including as the scent is particularly fine and long lasting.

Gloire de Guilan has double pink flowers which are very fragrant and forms a loose shrub which grows to 2 metres. It can also be used to make attar of roses but unfortunately it takes more than 100,000 flowers to make one kilogram.

York and Lancaster (Damascena Versicolor) This historic rose has semi-double flowers, some pink, some white and some a mixture of the two. It is very distinctive and well scented.

Leda or Painted Damask is a very fragrant rose with many petalled blush white flowers tinged with carmine red at the edges. It is the only damask rose which can sometimes bloom recurrently.

4. *The beautiful old Damask rose Madame Hardy.*

Alba Roses

Alba roses are robust hardy shrubs which are easily grown. These roses have softly coloured flowers with exquisite scent. They need light pruning only.

Célesté Charming pink double flowers. This rose is the origin of the term 'Celestial Pink'. It retains most of this colour when dried and has a fine scent. It grows to 2 metres.

Maiden's Blush (Great) the flowers are blush pink, double and very fragrant with grey green foliage. It grows to 2 metres.

Blush (Small) As above but with smaller flowers. Growth is limited to just over 1 metre.

Queen of Denmark has classic rose pink flowers, a very strong scent and grey green leaves. Grows to about 1.5 metres.

Maxima 'The Jacobite Rose' has creamy flowers, is very fragrant and semi-double. It grows to 2½ metres.

Félicité Parmentier has pale salmon-pink many petalled flowers which are strongly scented and shapely. The bush is upright and grows to 1½ metres.

5. *Alba roses provide a profusion of petals for potpourri.*

Bourbon Roses

These are generously scented and the flowers bloom recurrently. They are a predecessor of the modern Hybrid Tea. They need light pruning to keep them in shape and any spindly or dead wood should be cut out.

Commandant Beaurepaire has prolific flowers of pink, red and purple, striped, flecked and very fragrant. The foliage is light green and the plant grows to 1.5 metres.

Kathleen Harrop is fragrant with double pink flowers which bloom well into the autumn. This rose is thornless and grows to 2.5 metres.

La Reine Victoria has very double deep pink flowers which bloom over a long period with a warm scent. It grows to 1.5 metres.

Madame Isaac Pereire has generous flowers of deep rose magenta. They are wonderfully scented and the bush grows to 2.5 metres.

Souvenir de la Malmaison bears pale pink and very full blooms; these are quartered and heavily scented and they repeat well during the growing season. This rose matures to a shapely bush of about 1.5 metres.

Louise Odier. These beautifully full cup shaped flowers are pink with a touch of lavender and have an exquisite scent. This rose grows to 2 metres.

6. *The Bourbon rose 'Kathleen Harrop' provides fragrant pink petals for potpourri.*

6

Rugosa Roses

These are wonderfully generous roses which are resistant to disease. They will grow on the most difficult sites and most of them have a warm, rich scent. The bright green leaves turn gold in autumn.

Agnes has golden apricot double flowers. These are well scented and early flowering with a few late blooms. It forms a spreading bush of 1.5 metres.

Hansa produces large prolific, double flowers of a rich red violet colour. These are strongly scented and slightly recurrent with red hips in the autumn.

Roseraie de l' Hay has large, loosely double crimson, purple flowers which to my mind have the most wonderful scent of any rose.

Aloha

Aloha is a modern shrub rose which forms a large bush or pillar rose. It has enormous double pink blooms with a rich scent. These gorgous doubles are produced from June to November. One specimen of Aloha will give you an affluence of roses.

7. *The richly scented 'Aloha' flowers blend well with an old brick wall.*

7

Little White Pet

The China rose **Little White Pet** is a small bushy plant smothered in little blush white pom pom roses. These blooms can be dried whole (this takes about 8 days). Unlike most white roses the colour deepens to pink as it dries and the flowers retain their scent better than any other rose I know.

R. Eglantine

One rose and its hybrids have scented foliage – this is Rose Eglantine – the sweet briar. The large sprawling rose has clusters of small single pink flowers which later form bright scarlet hips. These are high in vitamin C and are used for making rose hip syrup. The leaves have a fresh apple like scent and dry well for use in potpourri.

Rose Eglantine is not suitable for a tidy garden. It is best grown naturally in an uncultivated spot and is sometimes found growing wild.

8. *The attractive rose Little White Pet, here grown as a standard.*

Hybrid Musk Roses

These charming delicate looking roses which form shapely mounds with sprays of softly-tinted blooms, are in fact very hardy. They will thrive in most conditions and are not prone to disease. Musk roses flower recurrently and are highly fragrant.

Buff Beauty is a sweetly scented rose which has fully, double, creamy apricot flowers. The petals retain their colour very well when dried as do most roses of similar colouring. It forms a bush of about 1.5 metres.

Cornelia produces prolific sprays of small apricot-pink flowers which are heavily scented. It grows to about 2 metres.

Felicia is a particularly attractive rose which bears a profusion of scented double pink flowers and attains a height of 1.5 metres.

Hybrid Perpetual Roses are vigorous and need to be pruned back hard each year. The flowers are very large and full and most have a strong scent.

Baroness Rothschild. Smothers itself with large pink roses which have a strong scent.

Ferdinand Pichard is an enchanting striped rose with a rich fragrance. The flowers are pink with crimson stripes splashed with white and repeat well into the autumn.

9. *The Hybrid Musk rose 'Buff Beauty' blooms profusely and is recurrent.*

9

Climbers & Ramblers

One well-established climbing or rambling rose can give enough petals to make a good quantity of potpourri and still leave a beautiful display of flowers on the bush.

Albertine is a very popular old rambler which grows to 5 metres. It bears deep salmon buds opening to fragrant, apricot peach flowers and has one generous flowering.

Blairi No. 2 grows to 5 metres with old rose pink, fully double flowers, which are very fragrant. It has one long annual flowering.

Climbing Souvenir de la Malmaison is similar to its parent (mentioned under Bourbon Roses). It grows to 4 metres.

Devoniensis reaches 4 metres bearing creamy white flowers tinged with peach. These are very fragrant and recurrent. This rose needs a sheltered sunny position.

Easlea's Golden Rambler grows to over 4 metres. The flowers are a rich golden yellow on long stems and are well scented.

Lavender Lassie grows to about 3 metres and can be left as a large sprawling shrub or trained as a climber. The flowers which are pink with a tinge of lavender, have a strong scent and are recurrent.

Madame Gregoire Stachelin is an old climbing Hybrid Tea rose. The richly fragrant flowers are large, soft pink and of classic H.T. shape. This rose will grow to 4 metres and has one very large annual crop of flowers.

10. Blairi No. 2 is beautiful in the garden and is useful for potpourri.

Moss Roses

These roses are so-called because of the 'mossy' growth on the stem, calyx and sepals of the plant. Some of this variety flower recurrently and most have a rich, old rose scent.

When pruning, these roses should be cut to about half their length for the single-flowering varieties; the recurring mosses need to be pruned vigorously.

Alfred de Dalmas has creamy-pink, double flowers which are very fragrant with some late blooms. The bush grows to just over one metre.

Capitaine John Ingram produces delightfully fragrant flowers of deep purple crimson with a button eye when fully open. The bush has dark, green foliage and grows to 1.5 metres.

Common Moss or Old Pink Moss. This well known variety has mossy buds opening to clear pink, fragrant flowers and grows to 1.5 metres.

William Lobb or Old Velvet Moss has dark, crimson double flowers which fade to deep lavender. The plant is heavily mossed and tall, growing to 1.5 metres. It becomes rather leggy with sparse foliage at the base and is best under-planted with bushy foliage plants such as Cotton Lavender or Artemesia.

Général Kléber grows to 1½ metres with plenty of moss on the buds which open to large rose pink quartered flowers with a button eye. This rose is strongly scented.

11. The Moss rose combines a Victorian appearance with a fine scent.

Lavender Lavandula Officinalis

This is an essential potpourri herb. All lavenders have aromatic foliage and lasting scented flowers. Lavender is traditionally used as an antiseptic. It is also reputed to soothe headaches and encourage sleep. It is a short lived shrub usually lasting about 6 years.

To enlarge your stock take heel cuttings from existing lavender bushes in July and set these into a sandy soil to root.

There are several varieties to choose from:

Hidcote has dark violet flower spikes with compact growth.

Munstead is similar to Hidcote but is slightly taller.

Nana Atropurea is a compact dwarf lavender with deep purple flowers and grey foliage.

Nana Rosea produces pale pink flowers with delicate silver foliage.

Spica is the old English lavender. It is a bushy plant with grey foliage and long flower spikes.

Vera was originally introduced by the Romans and it yields oil. The foliage is silver grey, and bushy. This is a particularly fine lavender for edging flower borders.

12. A well established lavender bush from which it is easy to take cuttings.

Other Flowers used in Potpourri

Clove Pinks have long been a favourite of the English pot-pourri makers. They can be dried whole and have a lasting scent. Also much used are Lily of The Valley and the honey-sweet scented flowers of **Prunus Lusitanica** (The Portugal Laurel) which flowers in June.

The flowers of Jasmine, Honeysuckle and 'The Tobacco Plant' with their haunting fragrance are best used in moist potpourri as they are unattractive when completely dry and lose much of their scent.

The flower heads of pink field clover dry well and keep a sweet scent reminiscent of hay. I particularly, like to use them in sleep-inducing potpourri.

Some flowers are used for colour rather then scent. An open bowl of potpourri is enhanced by the addition of rose buds, cornflower heads, delphiniums, marigolds or some bright tulip petals.

Violets are used in many old potpourri recipes which leads one to believe that in those days there must have been a violet with more scent. I find the present-day plants not only lose all scent when dried but also it is not easy to pick a pint of violets. Instead, violet oil can be obtained and added to the potpourri recipe.

13. *It is not essential to have a large garden to grow herbs. These are growing well in an old sink.*

13

Aromatic Plants for use in Potpourri

Artemisias: This group of plants are useful insect repellents, and the silver grey foliage looks very attractive planted among roses.

A. Pontica Roman Wormwood (Old Warrior): A. Pontica is a hardy perennial with fine grey fronds of aromatic foliage and small yellow grey flowers.

A. Abrotanum Southern Wood (Old Man or Lads Love): A. Abrotanum is a tall growing herb with grey-green foliage and small greenish flower spikes, these have a fruity scent. This plant is supposed to be a symbol of true love.

A. Absinthium Wormwood (Old Woman): This strongly aromatic plant has grey-green finely cut leaves and bears small yellow flowers in August.

Bay Laurus Nobilis: Bay Laurus Nobilis is a shrub growing to over 3 metres with dark green aromatic leaves which are much used in potpourri and cookery. It should be planted in a sheltered position as it is tender when young, but it becomes hardy with maturity.

Bergamot (Bee Balm): This hardy perennial grows up to 1.5 metres with decorative aromatic leaves and striking scarlet flowers.

Camphor Plant Balsamita Vulgaris: A hardy perennial growing to 1.5 metres with long pale grey-green coloured leaves which repel moths. When dried it has daisy like flowers and a strong refreshing scent. It is in fact so strong that it can take your breath away.

14. Artemisia bushes growing as part of a herb garden.

15. Chamomile will spread over paving stone to hide the straight edges.

14

15

Catmint Nepeta Mussinii: This herb grows to 1 metre high and about 2 metres across, it forms a sprawling evergreen bush with aromatic green-grey foliage and mauve flower spikes.

Catnip Nepeta Cataria: Catnip Nepeta Cataria also grows to 1 metre with soft green leaves and insignificant flowers in the late summer. Both Catnip and Catmint as the name suggests, are beloved of cats.

Chamomile Anthemis Nobilis: Chamomile Anthemis Nobilis is a low growing ground cover herb. It forms a green carpet with creamy white double flowers much used in potpourri.

Cotton Lavender Santolina: Cotton Lavender Santalina is a highly aromatic plant with grey lacy foliage. This plant forms a neat silver mound which is very attractive. It has yellow butter flowers. The leaves are used in potpourri, and may be substituted for lavender.

Eucalyptus Citriodorus: Eucalyptus Citriodorus is a small tree which is borderline hardy and needs to be planted in a sheltered spot. The greyish leaves smell strongly of lemon and retain their scent well when dried.

Hop Humulus Lupus: Hop Humulus Lupus is a rampant perennial climber. It is invasive and can sometimes be found growing wild. The shrub is sleep inducing and often used in herb pillows.

Lemon Balm Melissa Officinalis: Lemon Balm Melissa Officinalis is a hardy herb which forms a bushy plant growing to 1 metre with fresh green lemon scented leaves and white flowers in August. This plant likes some shade. There are also a varigated form which has green leaves blotched with gold.

16. Cotton Lavender grown amongst old roses makes attractive ground cover and hides the bare rose stems.

17. Lemon Balm can be planted beside a path so that when it is touched it will give off scent.

16

17

Lemon Verbena Lippia Citriodora: Lemon Verbena Citriodora is a half hardy perennial which should be taken indoors during the winter months and kept there until the threat of the frost is over. This plant grows to 2 metres with leaves that have a delightful fresh lemon scent which is retained when dried.

Marjoram Origanum: This group of plants is bushy, low growing and perennial which dry well for the use of potpourri and attract butterflies when in flower.

Origanum Vulgare Compactum: Origanum Vulgare Compactum is a small plant with bright green aromatic leaves and lilac pink flowers.

Origanum Majorana: Origanum Majorana is a half hardy perennial which needs to be taken in during the winter. It has silver-grey silky leaves and white flowers.

Meadowsweet Spirea Ulmaria: This plant grows to over 1 metre and likes damp soil. It has pinnate leaves and cream flowers in June and July which are sweetly scented. This plant was originally used as a strewing herb.

Mint Mentha: Mint Mentha is a hardy perennial which is easily grown and invasive. The best varieties for potpourri are Eau-de-cologne, Ginger, Lavender, Orange, Pineapple and Eucalyptus mint. The last has a peppermint scent, the others are named for their scents.

18. *Catmint can be invasive and is therefore best grown in a confined bed.*

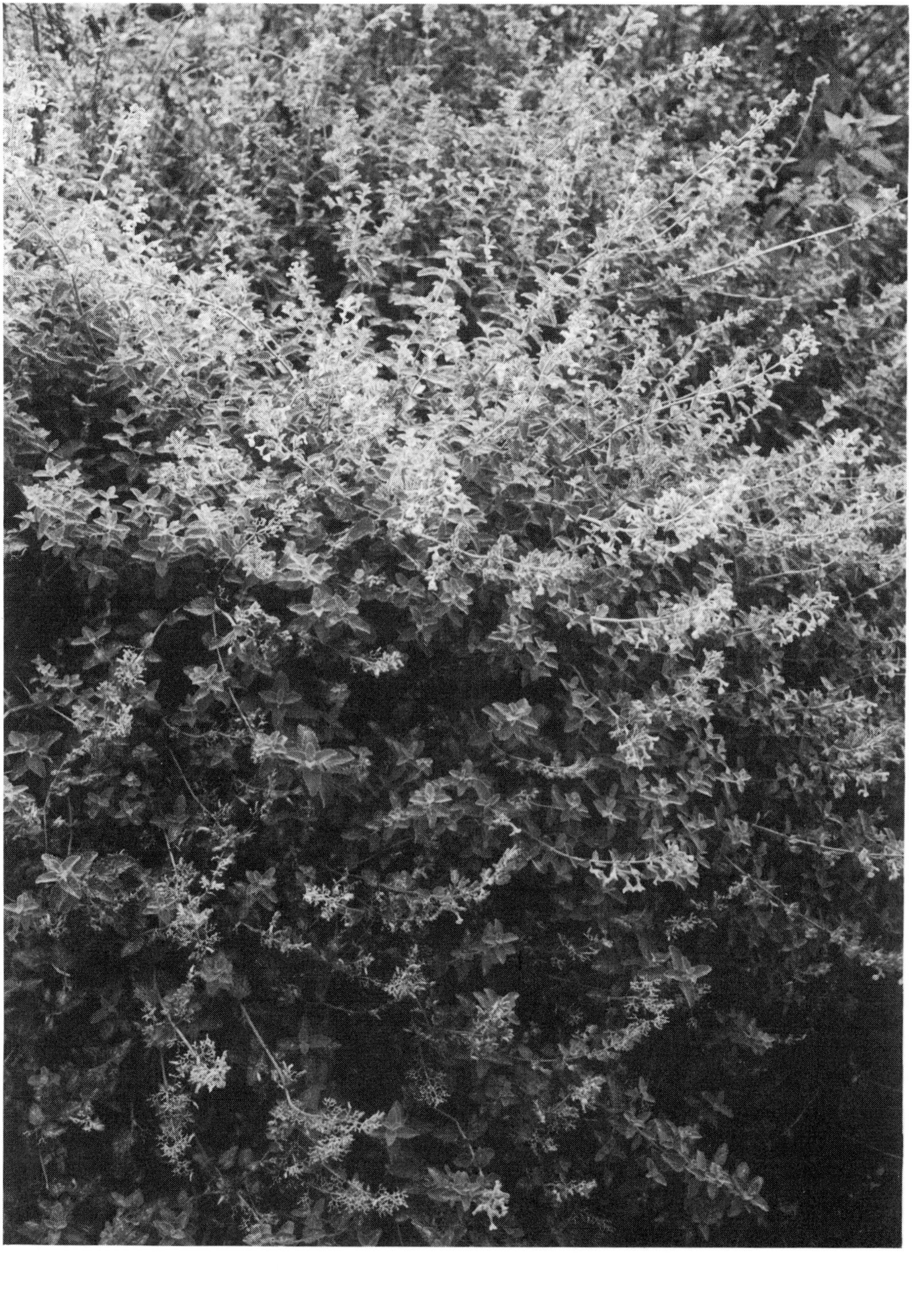

Myrtle Myrtus Communis: Myrtle Myrtus Communis is a borderline hardy, evergreen shrub with bright green aromatic leaves and fragrant white flowers in late summer. The oil extracted from the bark and leaves is used in perfumery.

Orris Iris Florentina: Orris Iris Florentina grows to one metre with pale mauve flowers. The dried, powdered root is the most popular fixative used in potpourri. Unfortunately, the root takes about two years to dry before it can be powdered. However powdered Orris may be bought from herbalists.

Pelargoniums: These ivy or scented leaved Geraniums are half-hardy perennials which make wonderful windowsill plants. If you brush against one, the scent will pervade the air. The leaves, when dried, retain their scent for two to three years and there are many delightfully-scented varieties from which to choose:-

Attar of Roses	Rose scented
Capittatum (Oak leaf Geranium)	Lemon Rose scented
Graveolens	Lemon scented
Crispum	Lemon scented
Denticulatum	Balsam scented
Filicfolium	Warm, musky scent
Royal Oak	Warm, musky scent
Fragrans	Spicy scent
Tomentosum	Peppermint scented

19. *Geranium plants and cuttings growing in pots on a windowsill.*

20. *A large selection of young herbs at Iden Croft Nurseries.*

19

20

Rosemary Rosmarinus Officinalis: Rosemary Rosmarinus Officinalis is an evergreen shrub which grows to over 1 metre and should be planted in a very sheltered position. It is borderline hardy and can be killed in a hard winter. It is a good idea to take cuttings each summer which will root quite easily in a sandy soil. It has pale lavender blue flowers and needle like leaves, with a lasting aromatic fragrance much used in potpourri as well as for cooking.

Valerian Valeriana Officinalis: Valerian Valeriana Officinalis is a herb with bushy green foliage and tiny pale lavender pink flower heads in bunches, with a sweet lasting fragrance.

21. A mature rosemary bush planted in the shelter of a yew hedge.

21

Gathering & Drying

Always pick the ingredients for dry potpourri on a fine day, after the dew has evaporated, but before the hot sun has wasted the natural oils, which are contained in the flower heads and leaves.

The flowers you choose should have opened for the first time that day. The scent will then be at its peak. Discard any imperfect petals as these will not dry well and may decay.

Dry the petals in a warm airy room and out of direct sunlight which would bleach the colours. If you intend to dry a small amount at a time lay the petals individually on cloth or paper (newspaper is excellent for this). Never use plastic because the drying petals stick to it and I cannot recommend net as I find that the petals get caught up in it.

A sheet is very useful to dry a large quantity of petals, and petals which have been picked dry should not mark it, but should leave some of their scent on the linen. (A bed made up with one of these scented sheets is a pleasure).

Rose petals take about five days to dry. This does vary with weather conditions so they need to be checked now and again. When ready they should feel and rustle like tissue paper.

Whole flowers such as the little pompom rose buds will take longer. Small amounts of petals laid out individually need not be touched, but large quantities of petals which overlap each other and whole flowers must be turned everyday.

When completely dry store the petals in an airtight container. I find old kitchen canisters useful for this.

22. *An old scullery such as this makes an ideal flower room.*

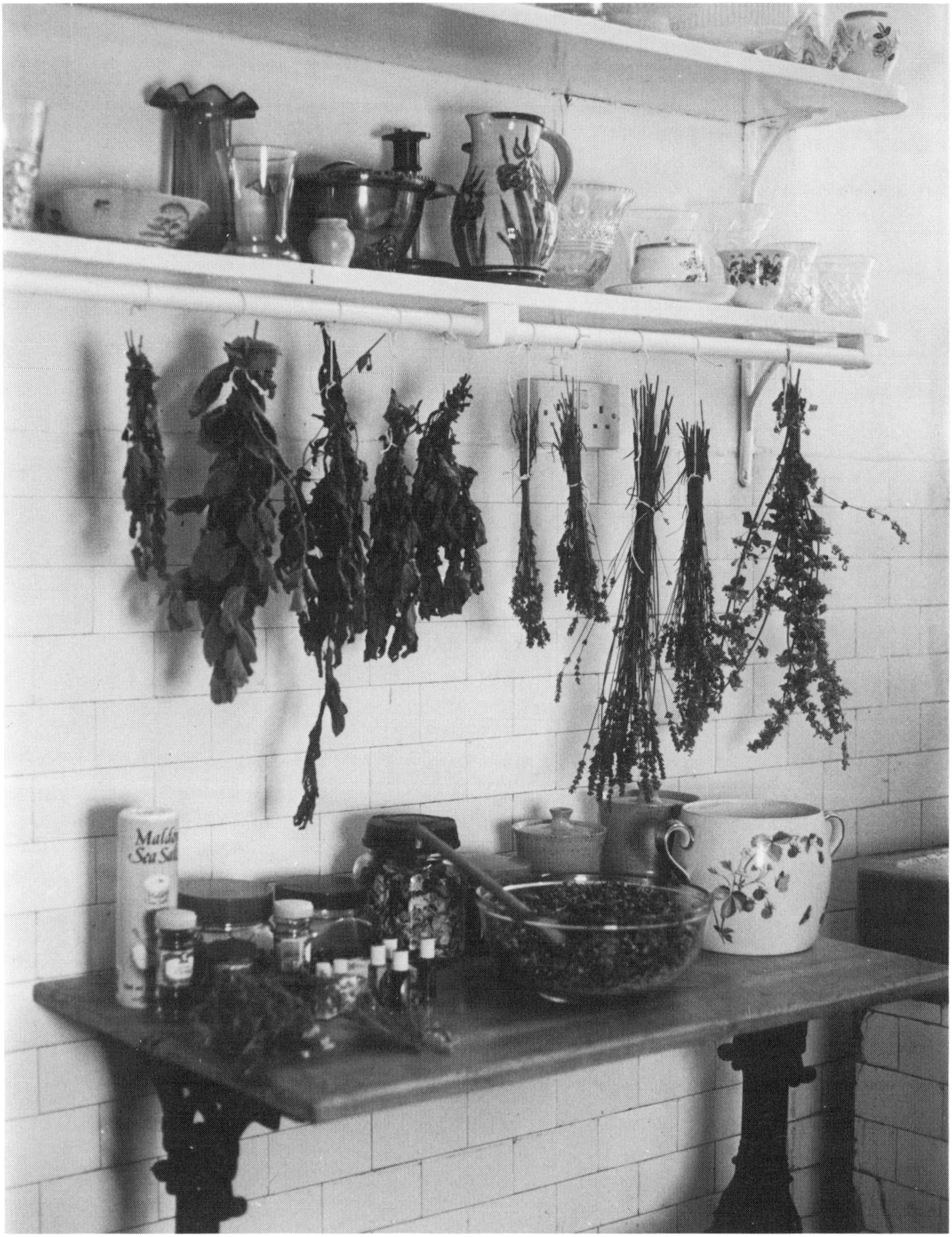

If you intend to make a lot of pot-pourri, place each type of flower in a separate container ready to be blended at a later time. The ingredients can then be stored until you have all the dried flowers you want.

Scented foliage dries easily. The leaves may be strewn over newspaper to dry or hung in bunches.

Citrus fruit peel with the pith removed may be dried and then finely chopped or minced.

Lavender should be picked just before the flowers open, and then hung to dry in bunches still on its stalks. When quite dry pull off the flower heads and store them.

23. *The ingredients for moist potpourri are simple and readily available.*

Moist Potpourri

Gather the flowers as you would for dry pot-pourri and strew them out thickly in order to partially dry them. This process takes about two days until the petals feel flabby and leathery. They must not become crisp.

There is a much wider variety of flowers which are suitable for moist potpourri. Some wonderfully scented flowers lose all their perfume when completely dry and just become ugly and shrivelled. I find tobacco flowers keep their delightful scent when partially dry as do most mockorange blossoms, honeysuckle and jasmine flowers. White rose petals which dry to an uninteresting biscuit colour are also best used in moist potpourri.

The moist potpourri recipes should be mixed directly the flowers are ready and not stored.

24. *A potpourri starter kit containing small amounts of all ingredients needed for dry potpourri.*

23

24

Drying in a microwave cooker

If you have a microwave cooker it is a very efficient and, of course, quick way of drying some whole flowers and herbs.

The pretty little rose buds which so enhance an open bowl of potpourri take about three minutes to dry. They also keep much more of their colour than by the slow drying method. Pompom and other fully double roses with short petals dry very well if picked half open. Carnations dry magnificently; they are best microwave dried before they are fully open and take about five minutes.

Heather dried on its stalk takes about three minutes and keeps its colour and shape so well that it is difficult to tell that it has been dried.

Lavender, catmint and herbs with small leaves such as rosemary left on the twig take about three minutes to dry, as do leaves and ornamental grass heads. When dried mix them with dried pink rose petals and clover heads and some wild rose buds to make a countryside potpourri. Add a few drops of meadow sweet oil and a tablespoon or orris root.

You can experiment in the microwave with flowers and leaves unsuitable to dry using the slow method. Little green fircones look lovely in a woodland potpourri as do green acorns. However I do not find a microwave cooker efficient for drying petals. They must be cooked separately otherwise they will congeal into one mass.

25. *Whole flowers retain more of their colour when dried in a microwave oven.*

25

Spices

These are very necessary in potpourri, both for their unique scent and because they help to fix the other scents used. They are easily obtainable from herbalists and grocers.

The most commonly used are cloves which can be whole or powdered, cinnamon, allspice, nutmeg and vanilla.

Fixatives

These are essential to fix the scented oils of the flowers and leaves used in potpourri, which would otherwise evaporate quickly. The one most used today is orris root (powdered or sliced). It has a slightly peppery scent. Use orris with care as too much can overpower the perfume mixture you have blended. Orris can be grown but the growing and the drying is a long process which takes a minimum of four years. In the meantime it can be obtained from a herbalist.

Sweet Flag may be substituted for orris. This will also grow in your garden.

Other fixatives are cedarwood, gum benzion, myrrh, patchauli, sandalwood in oil or powder form, tonka bean and vetiver. These are also obtainable from any herbalist.

26. *Some spices and fixatives are necessary in all potpourri recipes.*

26

Aromatic oils

These are used to strengthen the natural scent of the flowers which you have used in your potpourri mixture. On occasion they can be used to substitute for a flower you are unable to get, such as orange blossom or violets.

These oils may also be used to revitalise an old mixture.

There is a wonderful selection of oils to be obtained from a herbalist. They are also very strong so it is necessary to use them with care. Three or four drops is often quite enough.

It is possible to make your own oils but these will be nothing like as potent. The best method I have found is to soak your scented ingredients in pure oil for about one hour until saturated. Drain the excess oil off to use again, and place the flowers or foliage in the bottom of a large jar with a lid. Then sprinkle with salt to obtain one part of salt to six parts of flowers. Meanwhile more flowers should be put into the oil so that you can continue to make layers of oiled flowers and salt until all the oil is used. Seal the jar and leave it to mature for at least one month, stirring occasionally. As the contents mature the rather unpleasant oily scent will disappear and the flower scent emerge. When you are satisfied with the scent drain off the liquid, which will have formed, through a filter and into a bottle.

27. There are a great many aromatic oils available from which the potpourri maker can choose both for mixing and reviving potpourri.

27

Potpourri Recipes

The most exciting part of making potpourri is mixing the recipes – a blend of flowers and leaves producing a natural fragrance to suit your sense of smell and your memory. A bowl of potpourri may have the scent of a garden on a warm summer's day, a newly mown field or woodland in autumn.

I have listed some traditional and some new potpourri recipes which are worth trying. However before starting to mix be aware of one important caution: be very sparing when adding the fixatives and oils. It is very easy to add more to your mixture but it is impossible to remove an odour which overpowers the natural fragrance of the flowers.

28. *A chinese potpourri vase with attractive piercing to allow scent to escape.*

Rose Potpourri Traditional

4 pints Rose petals
2 pints Lavender flowers
1 pint Rosemary
1 pint Clove Pinks
1 pint Lemon Verbena
1 pint Violets (or 6 drops Violet Oil)
2 pints Sweet Briar Rose leaves
1 handful of Orris root finely chopped or ground
1 handful of crushed Cloves
1 handful of Allspice
6 drops of Damask Rose oil

Gently mix all the dry ingredients by hand in a large basin. Then drip in the oils and stir with a wooden spoon. Seal the mixture in a container for one month, which gives time for the scent to mature and blend. Unseal and add any extra oils or spices you think necessary.

28

A Rose Potpourri which includes Whole Flowers

This Mixture is suitable for display in open bowls. If you have a microwave cooker you can use it to dry the rosebuds and half open roses.

1 pint dried pink Rose petals
1 pint dried Lavender flowers
1 pint dried blue flower heads and petals (Delphinium, Cornflower, and Love-in-a-mist are very suitable)
½ pint dried pink Rose buds
½ pint whole Roses half open, use small many petaled roses
1 pint of dried Sweetbriar Rose leaves
1 tablespoon of Orris root
1 tablespoon of whole Cloves
8 drops of Rose oil

Mix all the ingredients gently so as not to break the whole flowers, then seal for 2 weeks in an airtight container to blend the scents. The mixture should than be ready for use.

If it is to stand in a large room with high ceilings it may be necessary to strengthen the scent with a few drops of lavender and clove oil as well as the rose oil. Potpourri in an open container will loose most of its scent after one season. It will be necessary to revitalise it with a few drops of aromatic oils. Do not use brandy to revive a dry potpourri mixture.

29. *This nineteenth century Minton bowl is ideal for displaying whole flower potpourris.*

29

A Simple Tranquil Potpourri Recipe

This potpourri is very suitable for scenting a bedroom. It can also be used in sleep cushions provided that the hops are broken up.

The recipe includes 4 drops of patchouli oil; but be very careful not to add too much of this voluptuous but invasive scent.

2 pints Hops
1 pint pink Clover heads
½ pint Lavender
¼ pint Rosemary
1 tablespoon Orris root powdered
1 tablespoon powdered Cloves
4 drops Patchouli oil

Combine all the dry ingredients and then add the 4 drops of oil and mix gently. Leave the mixture in a sealed container to blend the scents.

30. *A scented sleep cushion can be made to look attractive with appliqued decoration.*

Lavender & Herb Potpourri

This old aromatic herb potpourri mixture smells very refreshing and is particularly useful in a dining room or hall. It can be made to look more attractive by adding marigold and tulip petals.

2 pints of dried Lavender flowers
½ pint of dried Lemon Balm leaves
½ pint of Rosemary
½ pint of dried Chamomile flowers
½ pint of dried Thyme
1 pint of dried Pansy flowers
1 tablespoon each of powdered Cloves, Nutmeg, Allspice and Orris root
8 drops of Sweet Orange oil

Mix all the ingredients and leave covered for two weeks to blend.

31. *A silver potpourri box with a pierced top.*

30

31

A Fresh Scented Sachet Mixture

2 cups of dried scented Geranium leaves
2 cups of dried Lemon Verbena leaves
2 cups of dried Rosemary
3 dried Camphor leaves
6 drops of Bergamot oil

Crush all the dried ingredients to a coarse powder then add the bergamot oil and seal it in an airtight jar for 2 weeks to mature. It will then be ready for use.

32. *Sachets can be made in a great variety of shapes and sizes.*

Two Victorian Sachet Recipes
from *'The Wifes Own Book of Cookery'*

'A very pleasant perfume and also preventative against moths.

Take of cloves, caraway seeds, nutmeg, mace, cinnamon and toriquin beans of each one ounce; than add as much Florentine Orris root as will equal the other ingredients put together. Grind the whole well to powder and then put it in little bags among your clothes etc.

To Perfume Linen

Rose petals dried in the shade, or at about four feet from a stove – one pound. Of cloves, caraway seeds and allspice, of each one ounce; pound in a mortar or grind in a mill; dried salt, a quarter of a pound; mix all these together and put the compound into little bags'.

32

A Carnation Potpourri Mixture Using Whole Flowers

Whole carnation flowers can be dried in a microwave cooker which is most effective while losing very little of the colour. This handsome potpourri is suitable for a large open bowl.

1 pint of dried Carnations
1 pint of dried Clove Pinks
1 pint of dried Chamomile flowers
½ pint of dried scented Geranium leaves
1 handful of dried Bay leaves
1 tablespoon of whole Cloves
1 tablespoon of Allspice
1 tablespoon of Orris root
6 drops of Carnation oil

Mix the ingredients and seal for two weeks to allow the scents to blend. The potpourri is then ready for use but if it is used in an open bowl it will need to be revived from time to time.

33. *A Doulton spill vase with flower decoration here used as a small potpourri container.*

34. *An attractive oval bowl such as this looks well in a drawing room.*

34   33

An Old Moist Potpourri

'The Country Housewife's Book' contains a recipe for moist potpourri 'with one of the most delicious scents one can have in a room, never over-powering, but gently increases when the air of the room grows warmer'. This recipe is said to retain its fragrance for fifty years.

'Gather late in the day and when perfectly dry a peck of rose-petals, put them in a bowl and strew over them ¾ lb of common salt. Let them remain for 3 or 4 days and if more petals are added put in a little more salt.

Mix together a ¼ lb of bay salt, powdered cloves, allspice, and brown sugar also ¼ lb of gum benzoin, and powdered orris root. Add a gill of brandy and a few sprigs of lavender and scented verbena.

The mixture should occasionally be stirred but kept in covered jars; the covers only to be removed when the scent is wanted in the room. If after a time the mixture dries add a little more brandy'.

A second good recipe from the same book 'Pick all the petals available and perfumed sprigs as well, mixing rosemary and lavender with bay leaves, flowers of heliotrope mignonette and rose petals. Dry these a little with also some dried marjoram and lemon balm orange flowers if there are any. Put all into a china jar. Put in the peel of a sweet orange stuck with cloves, a few bits of stick cinnamon, sprinkle salt over and moisten from the top with a little brandy. Mix well together and keep closely covered when not wanted in use'.

35. *A good example of a modern potpourri bowl.*

36. *A 19th century Derby covered bowl for moist potpourri.*

35

36

A Rose Potpourri

A large and very fragrant recipe from '*Cre-Fydd's Family Fare or Young Housewifes Daily Assistant*'.

'Half a sack of rose leaves (petals), a quart of lavender, two ounces of sweet marjoram and two ounces of lemon thyme; spread these out on a table or a floor and turn them every day, till they are quite dry, when they will have shrunk to half the quantity. When dry, put them into a jar (or jars) and mix with them the following ingredients:- one ounce of gum benzain, one drachm of oil of cassia, one drachm of oil of cloves, two drachms of oil of lavender, one drachm of oil of cinnamon, a quarter of an ounce of bergamot, ten drops of oil of orange flowers, three ounces of Orris root, in fine powder, three quarters of a pound of dried salt, half an ounce of bay salt and two ounces of loaf sugar in fine powder; mix the ingredients well together, and cover the jar with a lid.

    Another mode may be adopted. Sprinkle the rose leaves with salt, and press them tightly down into the jar, and leave them for ten days then put them into a coarse cloth, and press out all the moisture. Pick the leaves apart, and finish in the same way as directed above. Will keep twenty years or longer'.

1 Drachm = 1 teaspoon

37. *This cut glass bowl is very suitable for whole flower mixtures.*

38. *Potpourri in a classic chinese bowl.*

37

38

Moist Rose and Pine Potpourri

This recipe has a beguiling scent reminiscent of some of the fine Scottish gardens, but it does not look very attractive and is best used in a tall slender container.

Eight cups of rose petals half-dried, four cups of pine needles which need not be dried and should be roughly chopped. Four cups of other fragrant flowers (half-dried tobacco flowers are excellent) and one cup of bergamot, a cup and a half of coarse salt and a cup and a half of fine salt.

Mix these ingredients thoroughly and put into a straight sided storage jar. Place a plate on top and weigh it down with a heavy object (an old lead weight is ideal) and seal it. The mixture must be left in the jar for four weeks. Open and stir thoroughly every two or three days. At the end of that time stir in eight drops of sandalwood oil and one tablespoon of gum benzoin.

Keep this potpourri covered when not in use.

39. A Wedgwood blue jasper covered urn suitable for moist potpourri.

39

Woodland Potpourri

Woodland potpourri makes an interesting change from the more usual flower based mixtures. It can combine that healthy 'woody' scent with a more masculine appeal, useful for halls, bathrooms and men's dressing rooms.

6 cups of dried Heather on the stalk
6 cups of pine and cedarwood chippings and bark left by the tree feller
2 cups of Rose hips
3 cups of dried scented Geranium leaves
2 cups of dried Rosemary on the stalk
2 dozen small fircones
The rind of three lemons with the pith removed cut into slivers
½ a cup of Cinnamon
½ a cup of Orris root
1 cup of coarse sea salt
12 drops of Sandalwood oil
12 drops of Juniper oil

This chunky potpourri looks very attractive in an old wooden bowl or barrel. Damp the inside of the barrel with 1 tablespoon of cherry brandy then put in the rest of the ingredients and stir gently. Leave the mixture covered for about one month stirring every other day. At the end of this time the scent should be fixed.

40. A finely grained wooden bowl such as this is ideal for woodland potpourri.

40

Using Potpourri

The earliest use of potpourri, and still probably the main use today, is to place it in containers about the house in order to keep a fresh and pleasant scent in all the rooms.

Bowls

Potpourri can of course be contained in any sort of bowl, provided the neck is not too tight. It is usual to choose a mixture for open bowls which not only has the necessary scent but also looks attractive; therefore the recipes containing whole heads of small flowers such as rosebuds and chamomile are the most popular for this use.

It is still quite possible to buy special potpourri containers which have pierced lids to allow the scent to escape. These were very popular during the 19th century and the early 20th century and a great many were made by the famous porcelain manufacturers of the time. They can still be found today in antique shops and at antique fairs.

Another antique container for potpourri, which is now quite rare, is the little silver box used by Victorian ladies to carry small amounts of the mixture in a pocket or a chatelaine. One can imagine that these gave a rather nice scent to clothes and if held for a moment in a pocket would also scent the hands. These boxes are quite rare and keenly collected by silver collectors, so the potpourri enthusiast would do well to buy one if the opportunity arises.

41. *An old Worcester bowl of the type much used for potpourri in the past.*

42. *A small pierced top potpourri bowl made early this century.*

43. *A chinese potpourri bowl.*

41

42 43

Baskets

Small baskets or woven rush containers look very natural filled with dry potpourri. They are inexpensive to buy or can be made at home. These baskets may be left open to show off an attractive mixture containing whole flowers and rose buds, or can be closed with a lid which may be decorated with dried flowers and leaves. The scent of the potpourri inside will be able to escape through the basket weave.

An open basket for use in a bedroom can be decorated with lace and have ribbon wound around the handle to give a more delicate effect.

Baskets used in this way should either have a solid wood bottom or be lined on the inside at the base to prevent powdered spices and fixatives falling through.

There are many other containers which can be used for potpourri, and the revived interest in country crafts and craft fairs makes a good area to seek for these. A few craftsmen are now making wooden gardeners' trugs for instance; a very small one of these can become an ideal container for potpourri to be placed in a garden room.

44. *Square basket with a solid wood base and lid.*

45. *A circular basket decorated for the bedroom.*

44

45

Cushions & Pillows

The most delightfully scented cushions and small pillows can be made up to hold potpourri which can be either mixed with the filling or inserted into the centre of the filling in a pad. I prefer to use the second method, as this can be renewed later when the scent has become weak, and also there is no danger of brittle pieces of flowers getting near to the surface of the cushion.

As these cushions are generally quite small it is usual to use a plain material or a material with a very small pattern. The quantity of cloth needed is also small so that the many off cuts of curtain and uphostery materials which tend to pile up in a drawer can at last be used. Some shops sell off their material samples as these go out of production; as a result it is sometimes possible to buy for very little, pieces of most exotic and costly materials which are quite large enough to make a cushion.

Scented cushions sometimes lend themselves to be attractively decorated and even a plain piece of material can be enhanced with flowers embroidered onto it. Another very effective treatment is to sew a lace mat onto the cushion so that the white lace gently contrasts with the colour of the material. Patchwork cushions are popular and they can, of course, be scented. Cushions can be made with frilly edges, edged with lace or decorated with piped or interlaced ribbons and all these and many others will be twice as attractive if they are also scented.

46. *Circular cushion decorated with lace and an old table mat.*

47. *A plain drawing room cushion.*

48. *A potpourri pillow for the bedroom.*

46

47

48

Lavender Bags and Sachets

Dried lavender flowers, scented geranium leaves and any other fresh smelling potpourri recipe can be made into sachets. Add one spoonful of powdered orris root to each pint of lavender flowers in order to obtain a longer lasting scent. You can use any scrap of light weight material you have handy to make up the little bags and also utilise any pieces of ribbon or lace as decoration.

There are of course many possible shapes which can be made. A little sack with a draw-string neck is very convenient so that the filling can be changed from time to time, and it can be made with a draw-string loop so that it can be attached to a clothes hanger. In order to obtain a perfect circle for a round sachet draw around a plate of the desired size. A heart shaped sachet is easily made if the material is folded in half before cutting out so that both sides are identical.

Camphor is an excellent moth repellent and the dried leaves of the camphor plant smell infinitely better than commercial moth balls. Dried cotton lavender and feverfew (chrysanthemum parthemium) are also effective against moths and leave a pleasant scent. A circle or square of muslin filled with one of these herbs and then tied tightly at the neck with ribbon or tape will make a useful moth repellent bag.

49. *A selection of potpourri sachets.*

50. *A covered clothes hanger with potpourri sachet attached.*

49

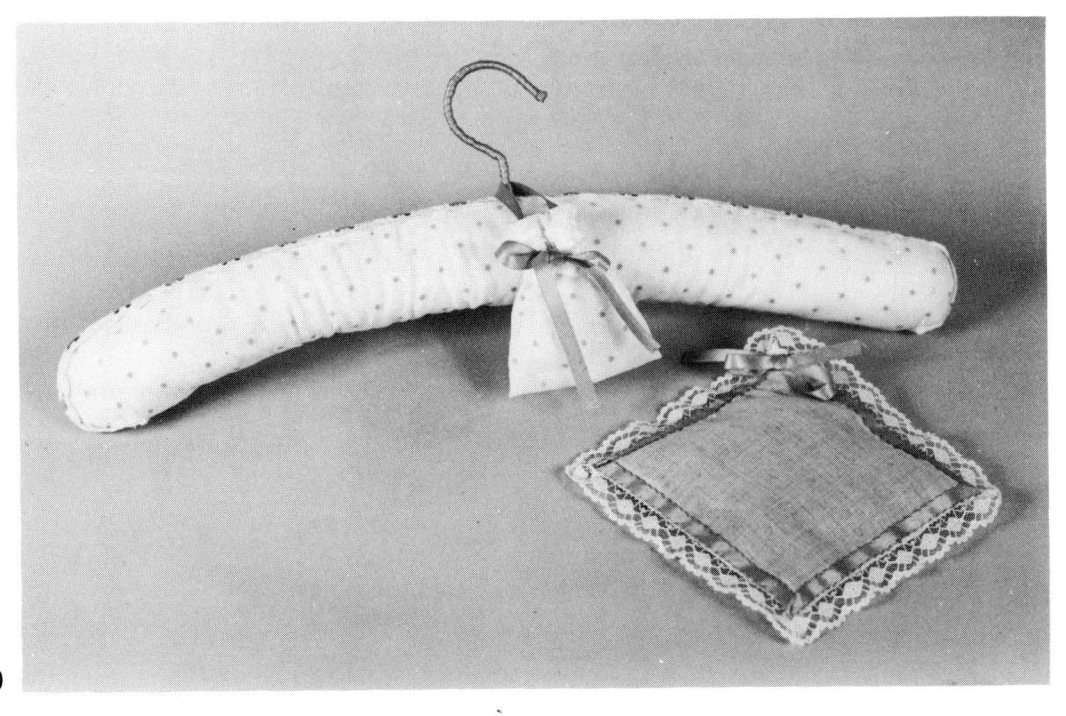

50

Catmint Bean Bags

Most cats love the scent of catmint or catnip. On warm days many a cat chooses to sleep in a nest he has made in the middle of a large catmint bush. He also likes to rub his face in it, eat it and roll in it. It is therefore good to be able to give him some of this pleasure in the winter time in the form of a catmint bean bag.

The dried catmint flowers and leaves should be mixed with some plastic 'beans', obtainable from most pet shops and used to stuff the bean bags.

These bags are very easy to make: two circles or squares of an equal size are cut out with a strip of the same material three or four inches wide to join the two together. The bag is then loosely filled with the catmint bean mixture so that when a cat climbs onto it he can sink into a 'nest'. Choose a strong hard wearing cloth for the bean bag as a contented cat will usually pummel the material using his claws.

51. The bean bag is filled with plastic beans and catmint.

51

Pomanders

Traditionally pomanders are made from an orange, pierced all over with cloves. In medieval times they used to be carried around by 'ladies of station' and occasionally sniffed as a guard against ill odours and plague. Today this would clearly look ridiculous, but they are very useful for hanging in a clothes cupboard or a bathroom to freshen the air.

In order to make a pomander you should partly dry a orange. A good way to do this is to hang it in the mesh sack in which it was bought in an airing cupboard or a warm place for a few weeks, until it is sufficiently dry not to rot.

Before inserting the cloves tie a ribbon or cord twice around the orange so as to quarter it and leave a large loop by which it can be hung up. The cord should be a dark colour as the orange will still ooze a little when the skin is pierced. Cover the remaining surface of the orange completely with dried cloves pierced into the skin. If you have trouble inserting them prick the holes first with a gimlet or steel knitting needle, so that the cloves slip in easily, but not so easily that they will fall out again.

Pomanders can also be made using a ball of 'florapac' or 'oasis' which is obtainable from most flower shops. With this juice free method any coloured ribbon or cord can be used and the cloves will be easy to insert. However it will be necessary to scent this pomander with some oil of sweet orange.

Both these pomanders can be revitalised from time to time with oil of sweet orange and clove. You should use just two or three drops, as a overscented pomander in a small room or cupboard can be quite over-powering.

52. The upper pomander is 'juice free' and has been decorated with ribbon. The lower one has been made using a real orange.

52

Scented Toys

It is quite surprising how children, and especially little girls, notice smells and scents. They quite often remark on them and, even when they do not make any comment, they recoil from something that smells musty or bad. It can therefore be a worthwhile idea to insert a scented sachet into a stuffed toy, and in order to help the child sleep well, to choose a tranquil potpourri mixture.

Be very sure that the sachet is placed deep into the stuffing and that the toy is properly sewn up, so that there is no possibility of it tearing open again, and insert a sachet which is too large for a child to swallow in the event of it being removed.

A good recipe for this is:

1 tablespoon of Lavender
1 tablespoon of Crushed Sweet Briar leaves
1 tablespoon of Damask Rose Petals
1 tablespoon of Chamomile
1 tablespoon of Lemon Balm
1 tablespoon of Valarium
2 drops of Damask Rose oil
2 drops of Sandalwood oil

53. This scented teddy bear will help a child to sleep well.

53

Car Freshener

While this sounds like a more modern use for potpourri in fact it would be surprising if lavender bags and pomanders were not sometimes carried in carriages during the nineteenth century.

Odours do persist in the enclosed atmosphere of a car and of course, so do pleasant scents. For lady's car a sachet filled with one of the rose based potpourris is very suitable, but for a man's car the smell of pine and sandlewood is more likely to be chosen.

For a ladies car I suggest:-

1 cup of Lemon Balm for the nerves
1 cup of Rosemary, to revive and stimulate
1 cup of Clove Pinks which have a wide awake scent

Mix these with 2 cups of Rose petals, 1 tablespoon of Orris root, 1 tablespoon of finely chopped lemon rind, 1 tablespoon of Cloves, and 4 drops of Damask Rose oil may be added if required.

For a man's car I suggest:-

1 cup Sweet Briar leaves to stimulate the nerves
1 cup of Rose scented Geranium leaves for remembrance
1 cup of chopped Pine needles
1 cup of Thyme which has a lively scent

Mix together with 1 tablespoon of Orris root, 1 tablespoon of grated Nutmeg and 4 drops of Sandalwood oil.

54. *A freshener can be any shape or size but should give the car a pleasant scent at all times.*

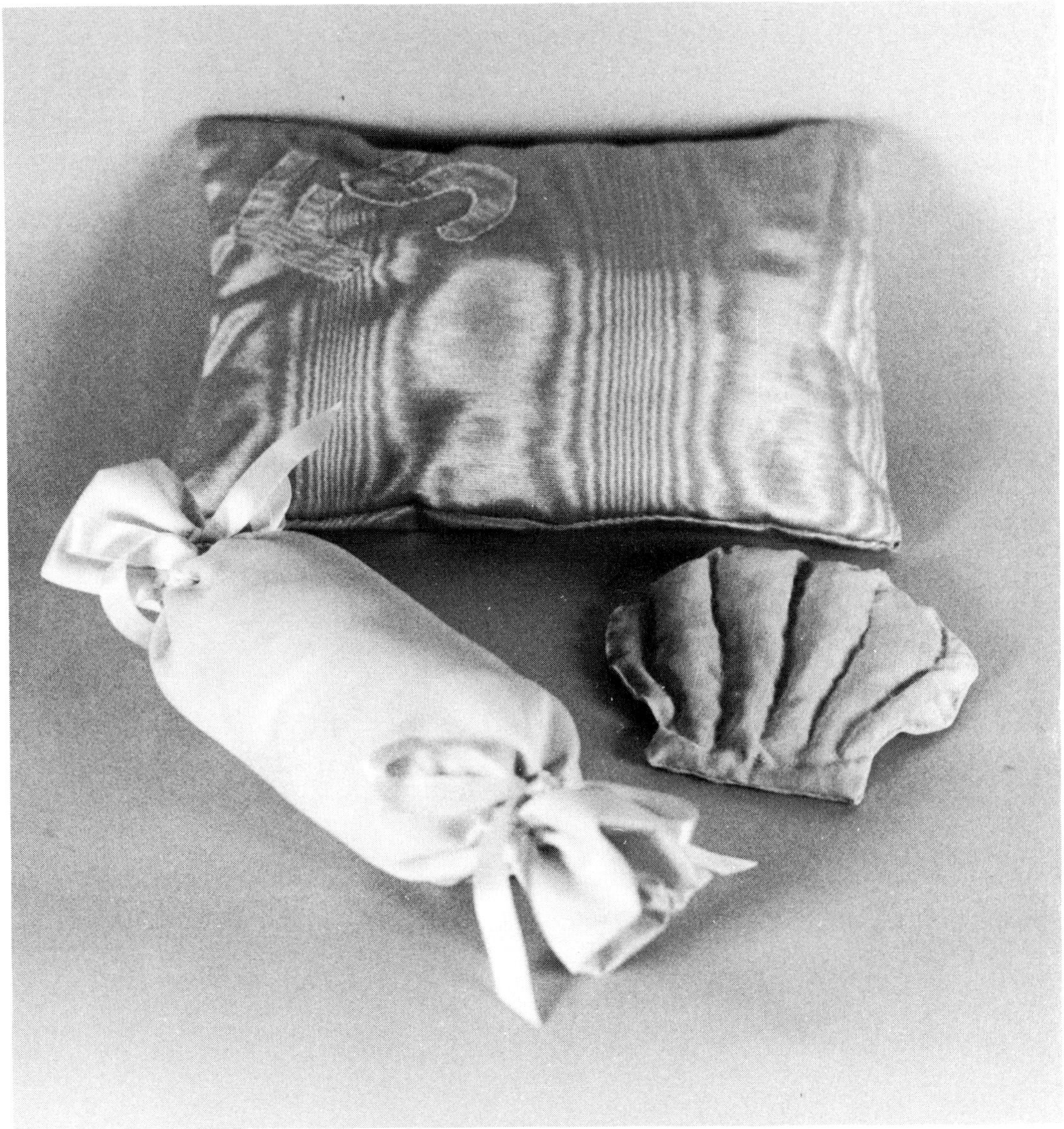

Flower Meanings

Over the years many flowers and herbs have come to symbolise a virtue or vice. The association of flower and meaning is in many cases based on sound common sense. Lavender for instance is, the flower symbol of purity and virtue, is an effective antiseptic.

This flower language was taken into consideration by the good wives blending their potpourri. A mixture for a sick person would contain tranquil and healing scents. A restful mixture for the bedroom, and a scented reminder of the rose and herbaceous borders to sweeten the winter air of the parlour.

These are some of the flowers and herbs most commonly used in potpourri together with their meanings.

55. *Dittany of Crete (13)*
    Aloe (14)
    Borage (15)
    Larch (16)
    Honeysuckle (17)
    Buckbean (18)

Anemone – Forsaken
Artemisia – Lovers fidelity
Arum Lily – Ardour
Balm – Healing and pleasantry
Basil – Hatred
Burage – Bluntness
Canterbury Bell – Constancy
Chamomile – Tranquillity
Clematis – Artifice
Cornflower – Delicacy
Clove Pink – Dignity
Daisy – Innocence
Daphne – Desire to please
Fennel – Strength
Heather – Solitude
Honeysuckle – Bond of love
Hop – Injustice
Jasmin – Amiability
Jonquille – Desire
Juniper – Asylum protection
Lavender – Purity, virtue and tranquillity

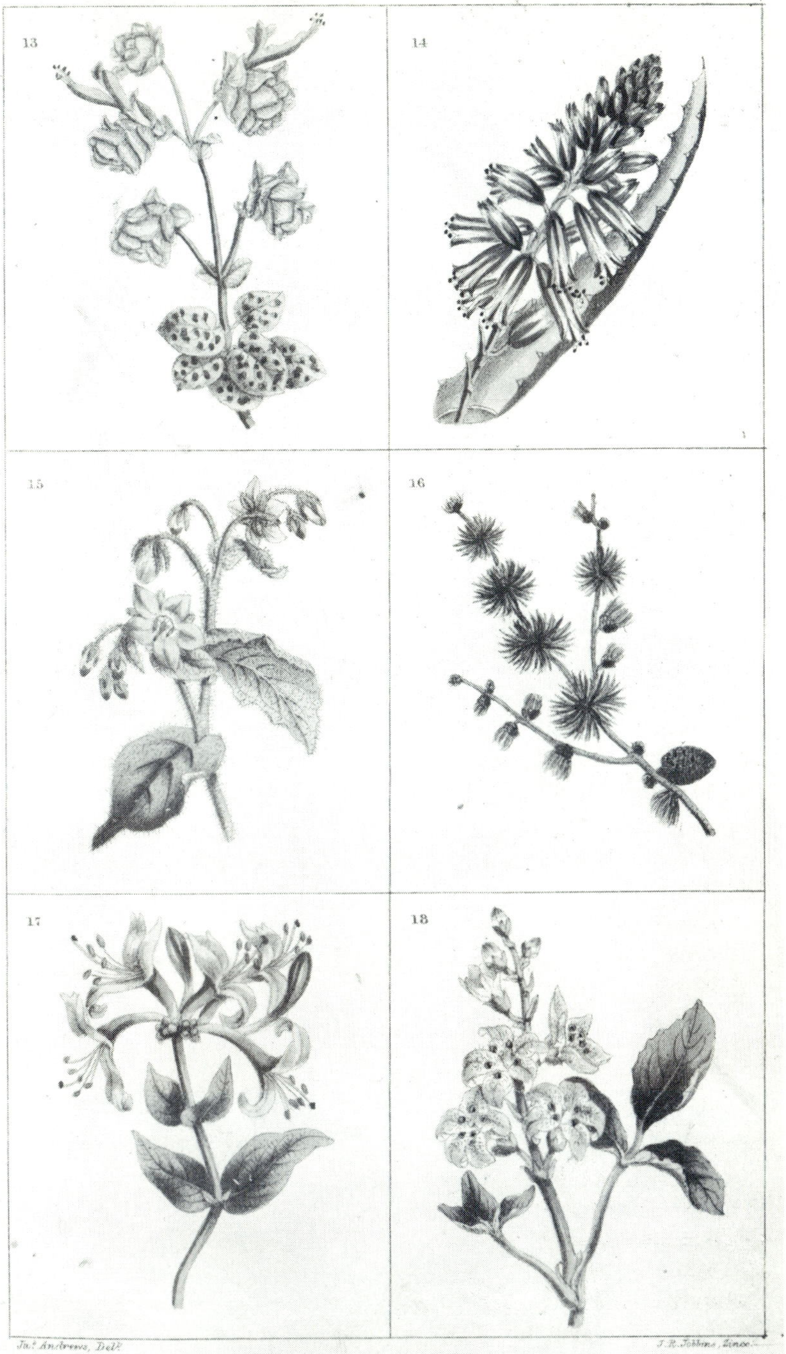

Jas. Andrews, Delt. J. R. Jobbins, Zinco.

Published by R. Tyas, 8, Paternoster Row, February, 1. 1841.

Lemon Balm – Soothing to the nerves
Lilac – First emotion of love
Lilac White – Youth
Lily – Purity and modesty
Lily of the Valley – Return of happiness
London Pride – Frivolity
Marigold – Despair
Michaelmas Daisy – Remembrance
Myrtle – Is dedicated to Venus, and is traditionally used in bridal flowers
Orange Flower – Chastity (also associated with brides)
Pansy or Hearts Ease – Think of me
Periwinkle – Sweet Remembrance
Pimpernel – Assignation
Pine – Elevation
Pink – Lively and pure affection
Poets Narcissus – Egotism
Rose – Beauty
Rose Monthly – Beauty ever new
Rose Moss – Pleasure without alloy
Rose Musk – Capricious beauty
Rose Provins – Graces
Rose Sweet Briar – Poetry a mental stimulant
Rose White – Silence
Rose Wild – Simplicity
Rose Yellow – Infidelity
Rose Bud – Young girl
Rose Bud White – The heart that knows not love
Rosemary – Your presence revives me, friendship
Rose Scented Geranium – Preference and remembrance
Sage – Esteem
Snowdrop – Consolation
Stock – Promptitude
Sweet William – Finesse
Thrift – Sympathy
Thyme – Activity
Tulip – Declaration of love
Valerian – Accommodating disposition

56. *Marvel of Peru (151)*
Agrimony (152)
Pansy (153)
Rock Madwort (154)
Spiderwort (155)
Bilberry (156)

56

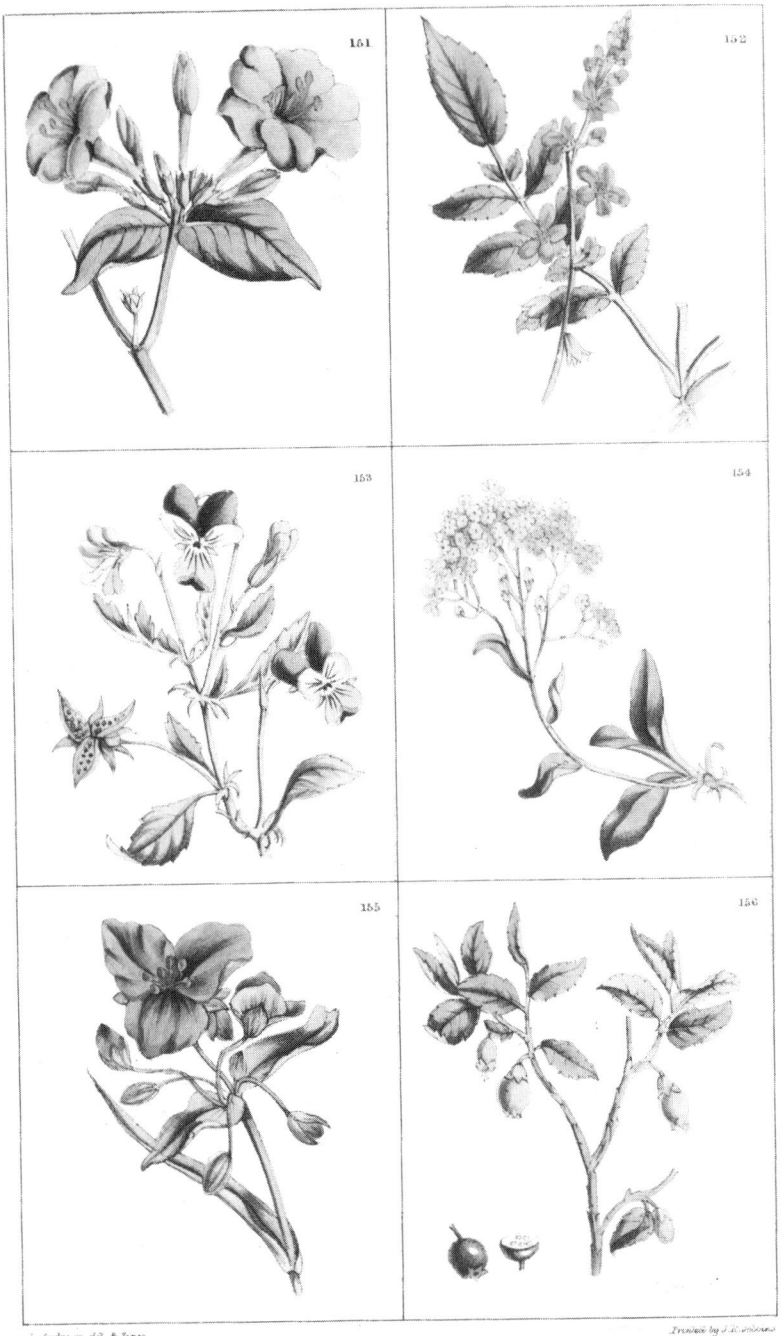

Vervain – Enchantment
Viburnum Tinus – I die if neglected
Violet Blue – Modesty
Violet White – Candour
Wall Flower – Fidelity in adversity
Wormwood – Absence
Yarrow – War

A Potpourri mixture containing Arum (ardour) Sweet Briar (mental stimulant) Fennel (strength) pine needles (elevation) Jonquille (desire) Rosemary (your presence revives me) and some Stock for (promptitude) should have a most invigorating effect!

57. Mignonette (163)
Rosemary (164)
Asiatic Ranunculus (165)
Pine Apple (166)
Anemone (167)
American Cowslip (168)

57

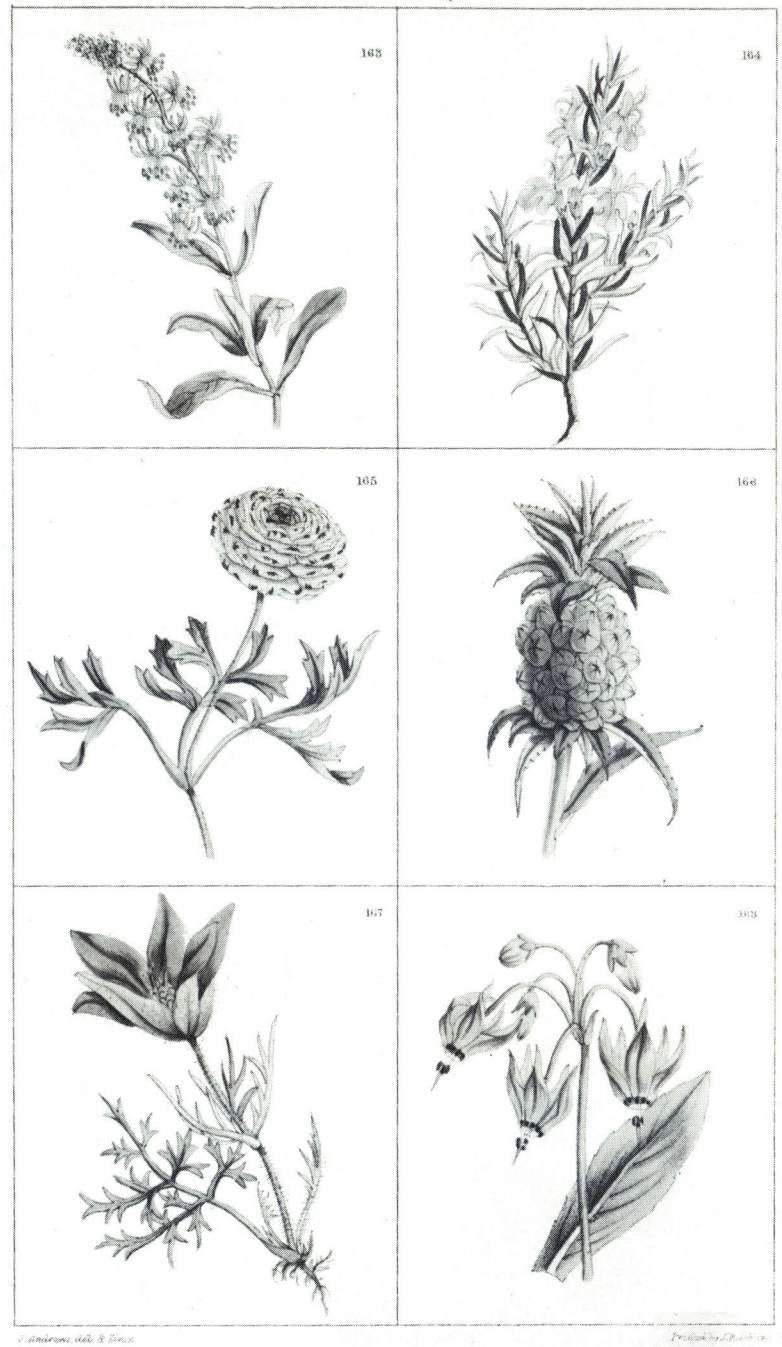

Reading

Potpourris and Other Fragrant Delights by Jacqueline Hériteau *(Penguin)*

Potpourri by Ann Tucker Fettner *(Hutchinson)*

Pot Pourri by Elizabeth Walker *(Darton, Longman & Todd)*

The Gardener's Book of Herbs by Mary Page *(Frederick Warne)*

Herb Gradens, Decorations, and Recipes by Emelie Tolley and Chris Mead *(Guild Publishing)*

The Book of Old Roses by Trevor Griffiths *(Mermaid Books)*

The Dictionary of Roses in Colour by S. Millan Gault & Patrick M. Synge *(Ebury Press & Michael Joseph)*

Cyril Fletcher's Rose Book *(Collins)*

Gardens for Small Country Houses by Gertrude Jekyll & Lawrence Weaver *(Hudson & Kearns)* originally published in 1912

We Made a Garden by Margery Fish *(David & Charles)*

Sentiment of Flowers by Robert Tyas originally published in 1862

Suppliers

Fixatives Oils and Resins

Meadon Herbs Ltd.
47 Morton Street,
London SW1

Culpeper Ltd.
21 Bruton Street,
London W1X 7DA

Old Rose Specialists

David Austin Roses
Bowlind Lane,
Albrighton,
Wolverhampton.

Peter Beales Roses
London Road,
Attleborough,
Norfolk.

Perry Hill Nurseries
Hartfield,
East Sussex.

Holkham Gardens
Holkham Park,
Wells, Norfolk.

(This walled nursery garden is covered by old climbing roses).

John Mattock Ltd.
Nuneham Courtenay,
Oxford.

Herb Specialists

Iden Croft Nurseries and Herb Farm
Frittenden Road,
Staplehurst,
Kent

Hollington Nurseries Ltd.
Woolton Hill,
Newbury,
Berks

The Cottage Herbery
Mill House,
Boraston Ford, Boraston,
Nr Tenbury Wells,
Worcestershire

Samares Herbs À Plenty
Samares Manor,
St Clement, Jersey,
Channel Islands

Pot Pourri Bowls

Michelle Ohlson
Chapel Studios
Stansfield,
Nr Clare, Suffolk

Trugs

The Truggery
Coopers Croft,
Herstmonceux,
Hailsham, Sussex

Gardens to Visit

The Royal Horticultural Society's Garden,
Wisley, Woking,
Surrey

The Royal National Rose Society Garden,
St Albans, Hertfordshire
(open to the public in June)

The Chelsea Physic Garden,
Fulham Palace Gdns,
London SW6

Michelham Priory Physic Garden,
Upper Dicker,
Nr Hailsham, East Sussex

Acorn Bank, (National Trust)
Temple Sowerby,
Cumbria
(A very fine herb garden)

Sissinghurst Castle Garden,
(National Trust)
Sissinghurst, Kent

Malleny Garden, (National Trust of
  Scotland)
Balerno, Scotland
(Large collection of shrub roses)

Botanic Gardens,
Glasgow,
Scotland

Arley Hall and Gardens,
Nr Northwich,
Cheshire
(includes shrub roses and herbs)

Hardwick Hall (National Trust)
Nr Chesterfield,
Derbyshire
(Extensive collection of herbs)

Cranborne Manor Gardens,
Dorset
(Herbs and specie roses)

Hidcote Manor Garden, (National Trust)
Nr Chipping Campden,
Gloucestershire

Kiftsgate Court,
Nr Chipping Campden,
Gloucestershire
(Specie and old fashioned roses)

Westbury Court Garden, (National Trust)
Westbury-on-Severn,
Gloucestershire
(Early formal garden)

Mottisfont Abbey, (National Trust)
Mottisfont, Hampshire
(Walled garden with old roses)

Eyhorne Manor,
Hollingbourne, Kent
(Herbs and old fashioned roses)

Lullingstone Castle
Eynsford, Kent
(Old roses, and herb garden under
  construction)

Gunby Hall, (National Trust)
Burgh-Le-Marsh,
Linconshire
(Walled gardens with roses and herbs)

Felbrigg Hall, (National Trust)
Nr Cromer, Norfolk
(Includes old walled garden)

Holdenby House Gardens,
Northampton
(Elizabethan scented garden)

Holme Pierrepont Hall,
Radcliffe-on-Trent,
Nottinghamshire
(Courtyard garden)

East Lambrook Manor
South Petherton,
Somerset
(Garden of the late Margery Fish)

The Herb Garden,
The Queens House,
Kew Gardens,
Richmond, Surrey

Queens Park,
Harborne,
Birmingham, Warwickshire
(Scented garden for the blind)

Parham,
Pulborough,
West Sussex
(Includes a herb garden)

Sheldon Manor,
Chippenham,
Wiltshire
(Fine collection of old fashioned roses).

OTHER TITLES IN THIS SERIES OF BOOKS:

RESTORING ANTIQUE FURNITURE
Richard Gethin

ISBN 0 900 873 31 0 (Cased)
ISBN 0 900 873 32 9 (Limp)

CANE AND RUSH SEATING
David and Freda Broan

ISBN 0 900 873 40 X (Cased)
ISBN 0 900 873 41 8 (Limp)

PICTURE FRAMING
Robert Self

ISBN 0 900 873 42 6 (Cased)
ISBN 0 900 873 43 X (Limp)

STRIPPING AND POLISHING FURNITURE
David Lawrence

ISBN 0 900 873 54 X (Cased)
ISBN 0 900 873 55 8 (Limp)

RESTORING OIL PAINTINGS
Tim Aldridge

ISBN 0 900 873 60 4 (Cased)
ISBN 0 900 873 62 0 (Limp)

UPHOLSTERY
David and Freda Broan

ISBN 0 900 873 48 5 (Cased)
ISBN 0 900 873 49 3 (Limp)

CHINA MENDING FOR BEGINNERS
Margot Wisler

ISBN 0 900 873 46 9 (Cased)
ISBN 0 900 873 47 7 (Limp)

RESTORING DOLLS
Doreen Perry

ISBN 0 900 873 59 0 (Cased)
ISBN 0 900 873 61 2 (Limp)

SPINNING AND WEAVING
Eileen Hobden

ISBN 0 900 873 68 4 (Cased)
ISBN 0 900 873 72 8 (Limp)